Redemption of a Rogue LAPD Cop

The Ruben Palomares Story

By Rayford L. Johnson

Copyright © 2017 By ThugExposed.Org

Table Of Contents

Special Note To Readers: **1**

Introduction: **3**

Chapter 1
East L.A. Hood Mentality: **4**

Chapter 2
Golden Gloves & An Olympic Hope: **9**

Chapter 3
LAPD, With a Mission to Save the Youth: **12**

Chapter 4:
Back to High School in South-Central Undercover: **15**

Chapter 5
Cursed by Witchcraft: **21**

Chapter 6:
The "Set Up"... Prison Bound: **24**

Chapter 7
Spiritual Warfare: **32**

Chapter 8
On the Path to God's Inner Healing & Demon Deliverance: **41**

Chapter 9
Ruben's Mission Now As A Free Man: **56**

Basic Prayer of Salvation & Deliverance: **58**

Redemption of a Rogue LAPD Cop

Special Note To The Reader

Ruben Palomares contacted me via email in the early part of 2017. In his email he conveyed that he had been praying and felt compelled by the Holy Spirit that it was time to share his story. He expressed to me that the real story behind the Hollywood themed sensationalism of his amazing testimonial, is that God loves us and wants to heal all our inner wounds, caused by the trauma of pain, fear, disappointments, violence, addictions, anger, neglect, rejection, and abuse that we have accumulated through our challenging life here on earth.

Surely he hath borne our griefs, and carried our sorrows: yet we did esteem him stricken, smitten of God, and afflicted.

But he was wounded for our transgressions, he was bruised for our iniquities: the chastisement of our peace was upon him; and with his stripes we are healed.
Isaiah 53: 4-5

After we spoke, I went into prayer myself about whether or not to publish his story. That week, God gave me a peace in my spirit to move ahead. From that point Ruben and I talked on the phone frequently about Biblical deliverance and inner-healing and how we believed the Holy Spirit would lead us to present this anointed story. Both of us being called into the ministry of healing and demon deliverance, we had some interesting and enlightening conversations, which was truly an ironing sharpening iron experience.

God used Ruben as he did my pastor, Fernando Perez, to take my position in the Deliverance and Healing Ministry to another level. God has given Ruben a powerful anointing and wisdom in addressing inner-healing. Many times before I pray for an individual for demon deliverance and inner-healing, I have them read or watch Ruben's anointed testimonial story first.

My prayer is for the reader to gain an understanding and a strong faith through the anointed knowledge and wisdom of Ruben's story, so that they too may experience the peace and joy that comes only through the inner-healing gift of Yeshua Hamashia (Jesus Christ).

God Bless,
Brotha Ray

ThugExposed.Org Ministry Director

Introduction

As I sit across from Ruben Palomares for this exclusive ThugExposed.Org interview, he has only two days left before he comes off house supervision.

Ruben was just recently released from serving more than 16 years in a federal prison for being a ringleader of a gang of rogue Los Angeles Police Department (LAPD) cops who were doing home invasion robberies and collecting debts for the Mexican Cartel among other criminal activities.

Ruben conveyed to me that he felt compelled by the Holy Spirit to contact ThugExposed.Org Ministries to share his story. It is an amazing true story which would appear too hard for even Hollywood to embellish and believe. His story reads like the movie, "Training Day," which starred Denzel Washington, but on steroids.

Chapter 1

East L.A. Hood Mentality

Ruben Palomares was born in Jalisco, Mexico and then his family moved to East Los Angeles when he was a one-year-old. He was raised up in poverty with 10 brothers and sisters with an alcoholic father who was both verbally and physically abusive.

"You're growing up in an environment where everybody has that tough guy attitude," he explained.

Ruben grew up in a gang infested neighborhood and around gang related uncles. I'll let him tell his story now in his own words:

"They (uncles) were gang members from Watts, they were way older than me, they were in a sense my role models. They would always try to instill some of their street belief systems in me. I was a kid. I remember being 5,6,7 years old, they already started brainwashing me with the mentality of never backing down, never let no one disrespect you, they instilled this evil pride inside me, that made me believe that I could not back out of a fight, no matter who disrespected me or bullied me or punked me, or tried to; I had to stand up and beat them."

"When I would go to T.J. (Tijuana), to Mexico, they would have pig pens, they would have me fight with my other uncles or cousins who were my age or older and just wrestle and fight until somebody tapped, we were just little kids. They enjoyed watching it and I couldn't back out of it, because to me, I had to let them know I wasn't afraid. I was their entertainment."

Ruben liked the accolades he received from his uncles for his tough and aggressive fighting mentality, however, reflecting back, he states, "It's really about being wise and learning how to walk away, but I was never taught that growing up."

"In elementary and junior high, high school, if anybody tried to disrespect me, if it was one guy, two, three guys, I would stand up for myself. I would fight two to three guys at a time, even if they jumped me and beat me up, I wouldn't back out. My friends would watch the rage come out of me, the rage that was so destructive, because I would start cussing and start saying some stuff like, "I'm going to kill you, and I would say some evil, nasty stuff that it would scare my friends and they wouldn't even want to jump in to help me."

"I never liked the gang structure mentality. I felt growing up as a kid, that teaming up, feeling confident that you got a bunch of homeboys to help you, I didn't believe in that stuff, I thought that was being more like afraid to be your own man and fight for yourself. So in my mind, I didn't want to be a part of that. I didn't want to be part of a structure where somebody is telling me how to be, how to live."

Ruben traces a lot of his anger and bitterness he had harbored within, back to his alcoholic stepfather. There was a hurtful surprise waiting for Ruben at the age of 17, which would inflict even deeper inner wounds into an already emotionally injured soul.

Ruben recounts, "I didn't know he was a stepdad until I was 17. He married my mom when she was already pregnant. I could feel the favoritism between me and my brothers and sisters, that started making me feel rejected. From that rejection I started to feel a lot of anger."

"He was drinking and he said, 'hey I want to tell you something. You're not my son, but I love you like my son.' I ignored him, I said 'you're drunk, you don't know what you're talking about.' I was just thinking he's drunk, just saying nonsense."

"But that day my mom was in the kitchen listening. She called me to the kitchen, she said, 'What's your dad telling you?' I said, 'Mom he's drunk. Well he's saying he's not my dad.'"

"I'm 17 years old at the time, I'm actually training for the Olympic team for 1988. So I'm not trying to get involved in nothing and get distracted by things. But then she starts crying, she says, 'What if I told you that it's true?' and she's got tears in her eyes. I said, "You know what? I don't want to hear that right now. So I just ignored it. I got bothered by it and just walked away. I suppressed it, I just held it inside.

"Even though he was abusive in the way he was, I still had this love for him, but I had this hatred for him too, I felt sorry for him too. I would see him drinking, I would see him drunk. That addiction had him.

Even though I wanted to beat him sometimes, the other side didn't want to beat him because I saw how weak he was, because of the addiction."

Chapter 2

Golden Gloves & An Olympic Hope

As a pre-teen, being the second oldest of his 10 siblings, Ruben began cultivating a good work ethic while doing construction with his uncles under the table for $20 a week. It was necessary for his mom to work, because his stepdad would often spend the bill money on alcohol. That work ethic would later work to his advantage as he would discipline himself to evolve into a Golden Gloves boxer and martial artist.

Still thirsting for genuine acceptance and love, which he was not getting at home, Ruben attempted to fill this void through his natural athleticism. "I learned to use my gifts in sports, to build an image for myself. In that mentality, I was somebody."

"Boxing was my number one love back then. I loved boxing because it gave me discipline, it taught me how to fight, it helped me to learn to respect myself and respect others at the same time."

At age 15, Ruben was already training hard for the

Golden Gloves title in California. "To get up in the morning, to go jogging in that environment, I would have to have a little .25 pistol on me. I would put it in my sleeve and I'm jogging by myself, I'm getting ready for the fighting, so I'm not trying to get shot or trying to get robbed or mugged or get beat up by some weirdo out there.

"I knew a lot of neighborhoods, Florencia (Florencia 13 Gang), I boxed in the projects. They liked me because I was the young Mexican kid coming up in the boxing world, they respected me and I had access to stuff if I needed it."

Ruben moved up the ladder in boxing quickly to the level where he became sparring partners with such boxing legends as Oscar De La Hoya and Sugar Shane Mosley.

His boxing dreams came crashing down when he was disqualified from the 1988 Olympics, due to his citizenship status of being born in Mexico.

He would make another attempt at his dream in 1991, training for the 1992 Olympics, but was injured while training for the trials. Ruben would then leave boxing for good.

"I left it alone, because I knew I wanted the gold medal. The gold medal was more important to me than to turn pro and work my way up as a pro, and go through the sharks. There is so much corruption in boxing and politics, it's bad. I didn't want to have to work my way up there and bleed too much, just to get a title belt and then end up messed up in your head from all the boxing."

Chapter 3

LAPD, With a Mission to Save the Youth

"So my next goal was to become a police officer with LAPD. I grew up in an environment where I saw cousins, friends and uncles get killed from gangs or drugs. I had an uncle when I was like 10 or 11 years old, he was like my favorite uncle, he got killed because he was a drug dealer from TJ (Tijuana). He ended up getting set up by somebody for two kilos of cocaine. It affected me bad, it made me hate drug dealers."

When asked how his family and friends felt about him becoming a police officer he told me, "Everybody was happy, because I was succeeding. I was doing something positive; I was accomplishing my goals, I was focused. I wanted to do something positive. I wanted to help people. I always enjoyed helping people, it was natural to me."

Ruben credits his old childhood boxing coach for inspiring him to want to be a police officer.

"Al Spanky was a retired police officer. I learned from

him, he was a good coach, he mentored a lot of the kids in the intercity in East L.A., that's where I trained, in Boyle Heights.

He would get us as young kids and take care of us; he respected us, he showed that he cared for us. Of course he cared about our skills too, because if you were a good boxer, he's going to take care of you even more. But I still enjoyed the fact that this person was there and he took the time to take us to our fights, take us training, running, you name it, he was there for us. So to me as a retired cop, he had a lot of influence over us, and we respected him.

So in my mind I'm thinking, I could become a police officer and go back in the neighborhoods I grew up in and give back, help these youngsters so they don't take that left turn to join a gang and get in that dope game and get themselves caught up and get themselves killed or put in prison."

Ruben began building his resume to be a police officer by working in security as a bodyguard. As an Olympic hopeful, Ruben was able to rub shoulders with the elite of Hollywood and professional sports. He did bodyguard work for high profile celebrities such as Arnold Schwarzenegger and Muhammad Ali and even worked for private investigators.

Chapter 4

Back to High School in South-Central Undercover

In 1993, Ruben passed the entrance exam and was hired by the Los Angeles Police Department. He easily excelled in the police academy's rigorous fitness exam due to his past conditioning as a Golden Gloves boxer. Having a very youthful appearance coming out of the academy, LAPD would capitalize on that.

"I wanted to go to South Central and work patrol. I was there for like six months. While there, they recruited me to work in the undercover high school program, it was like 21 Jump Street (the 1980s TV show). They sent me back to high school. I'm in the 11th grade, I'm already 23 years old. I got to fit in. I got to blend in. I got to play the part. Because what they want you to do is, infiltrate to find out where these kids are getting the drugs from, to lead you to the big suppliers.

So I'm in this high school and I'm buying drugs, getting intel and at one point I'm supposed to buy some PCP from one of the kids. He sets up a night to sell me the drugs."

That night Ruben gets notification on his pager, so he goes to a street phone booth to make the call.

"When I'm on the phone, these two older gang members try to rob me, and I get into a shootout with them. I end up getting shot in both of my legs. I end up shooting the guy, it becomes a big shoot out. Praise God I made it through that."

Self Medicating Anger, Bitterness & PTSD (Post Traumatic Stress Disorder)

The traumatic impact of the shooting would set in motion an entire new direction in Ruben's life.

"What the Department failed to realize, is that those type of shootings really impact a person. Mentally and emotionally I was messed up. It messes with your head, you have nightmares and flashbacks. You think everyone's got a gun, you think everybody out there is out to rob you, or shoot you. You don't have no peace, you don't rest. You start holding hatred towards people."

Redemption of a Rogue LAPD Cop

Ruben's past dysfunctional and traumatic childhood such as; break up of the marriage of his childhood sweetheart, compiled with the shooting incident, lead to what would later be diagnosed by mental health clinicians as PTSD (Post Traumatic Stress Disorder). Ruben explains:

"It starts from childhood, whatever you've seen or experienced-- my uncle getting killed, abuse, the drugs, the gangs-- and you're holding on to all that, gangs members putting guns to your head, neglect and rejection at home, you accumulate all that."

Feeling overwhelmed and depressed, Ruben starts self-medicating his PTSD with drugs and alcohol. He began drinking heavily, to the extent of putting away a fifth of vodka a day. He was taking pain pills and smoking marijuana. This in turn leads him down a very dark, demonic path, which would continue to get darker.

In 1995, Ruben transferred to the Rampart Division, where he would do undercover work for the Gang Task Force. He received rave reviews up until 1998. One captain wrote, "A leader with a reputation of excellence." Another said, "Another year of stellar service."

Going Rogue with the Mexican Cartel

It would take just one more traumatic event for Ruben to finally snap mentally and evolve into a person he didn't even recognize, or like.

"One of my partners got killed. I started thinking how the Department treats the family. I'm justifying everything. This Department doesn't know how it feels to be there (out in) the field dealing with all the gangs and all the violence. I started thinking about how the gang members were making $1 million a month in drugs, extortion, etc..

"I'm putting my life on the line, I'm working my butt off all these years and I'm still struggling. I'm thinking money will fix my problems at home."

The series of traumatic events, lead Ruben to a thought process of vigilante justifications, which triggered a meltdown, which eventually gave birth to a rogue cop mentality.

"I said, 'I'm going to start jacking these dudes.' I'm going to start going out there and getting some connections. I had already started establishing connections with some of the drug dealers out there. Immediately I started talking to some people, I said, 'Hey look, here's what I want to do, but keep it to yourself. If you have a debt you want me to collect, but it has to be in the mills (millions) and up.'"

I asked Ruben how he was able to get these guys to trust him, knowing he was a cop. He said that one of his drug connections was an individual he had grown up with in East L.A. Ruben said it took some persuasion. I asked him, 'What did you say to him?' Ruben described the guy acting as if he was in shock when he first propositioned him. Ruben said he told the guy the following: "I'm serious, but we got to look out for each other." The individual then responded, "I'll look into it," but he was freaking out at first."

"Once I did gain his trust, it was easier, because then he started reaching out to his connections and they ended up getting the first job for me."

Ruben had a plan to not only share the wealth with his fellow LAPD comrades, but to also build an inner gang or mafia within the ranks.

"I went then to talk to a few of my partners who were cops. I convinced them that we were going to collect a debt and it was illegal of course, but I thought these guys (gang members and drug dealers) weren't victims."

Ruben's crew of rogue cops pulled off over 40 home invasion robberies on the Mexican Cartel's competition, sometimes utilizing police cars they stole from the LAPD Police Academy. They would make the robberies look like legitimate Gang Task Force drug raids.

Chapter 5

Cursed by Witchcraft

The Mexican Cartel has a rooted connection to the ancestry witchcraft of Mexico. Ruben will now discuss how the cartel utilizes witches for intel and counsel against their competitors.

"Let's say you have a cartel guy who has "beef" with someone else, or even a girlfriend or a guy. They'll go to a witch. They'll get a picture from them (their victim), or get some hair from them, and give it to the witch. Then the witch would do their little rituals, whatever the process is, and they'll put a curse on the person. They can put a curse for death, they could put a curse for different reasons, to be sprung, etc... Some way off-the-wall stuff, but it actually really is real."

"One time I was working patrol, I was working the gang unit, this witch, she worked for 18th Street, she had her own little botanic (herbalist) store in the neighborhood. Well, she gave me some cards of the Arch Angel Michael with a prayer. What I didn't know

Redemption of a Rogue LAPD Cop

Arch Angel Michael with a prayer. What I didn't know until later on, was that she had cursed these cards. So when the cops take them, they go under the curse that she put on them. I got cursed by her and (so did a) few other officers who I gave them to."

Ruben's business ventures with the Mexican Cartel would inevitably lead him down an even darker cursed trail of witchcraft.

"I was still robbing these connections. I was taking down the cartel connections, I was actually taking down the competition for them and collecting debt for some of these guys. One of the guys who worked for me would always go to a witch, he would always invite me, I would say 'no'. He would say, 'come on man let's go to my witch.' The last time we went to take a house down, he wouldn't go with me, I asked why not? He said, "I went to my witch. She said for me not to go, but you guys are good.' I said 'You're going to believe all that stuff? You're crazy man, don't waste your time on that,' I didn't believe him."

"Just so he would leave me alone, so he could stop bugging me, I said, 'I'm going to go with you, let's go,' So we went to this witch in the East L.A. area. So when we show up, I go to her first. She has a room,

I sit out in front of her, she has a table, she pulls out her cards and then she reads my palm. And then she tells me, 'someone cursed you, someone put a death curse on you.' I say, 'What does that mean?' She says, 'They got sand or dirt from the cemetery, put it in a container, and they did this whole thing (ritual) on you and put a bad curse on you.'"

"I'm just listening, and then she says, 'also I see you're going to get a surgery and it's not going to come out right.' I had no intentions or plans to have surgery, none of that was in my mind. Then she says, 'I also see you in jail, prison,' and I'm like 'whatever.' She says, 'I can help you, but you got to do this, you got do that.' I basically played the part, but I never listened to her. I'm just thinking this all fake, so I didn't follow nothing. Reflecting back today, Ruben says, 'Thank God I didn't listen to her, because I would've got myself into more curses.'

"In the process of time working for the Police Department, I'm an instructor for the Department of Tactics and Self Defense. I end up getting injured in my shoulder (rotator cuff tears). When they went to do surgery, it was unsuccessful. The surgery came out bad. "Then after that, I get arrested."

Chapter 6

The "Set Up"... Prison Bound

"I get set up because my cousin is dealing with some Colombians in San Diego and they're going to go and buy 10 "keys"(kilograms) of cocaine off these guys. One of the guys asks if he can borrow a $100,000 from me, because he wants to buy the 10 keys. I end up lending the money, but also he ends up convincing me that this guy wants to hire me to collect a debt for him. So there I go like a dummy to go meet the Colombian connection. While we're there talking to him, we're about to leave the parking structure in Chula Vista, it's a sting operation, they take us down right there for the 10 keys of cocaine."

Ruben is convicted of being an admitted mastermind of a violent band of rogue officers and others who committed a string of armed robberies across Southern California staged to look like law enforcement raids. He was sentenced to 13 years in federal prison, coupled with a related drug case, which totaled 16 years.

Redemption of a Rogue LAPD Cop

"My mentality was, I got busted, I'm ready to go hard and in my head I'm all thinking, first guy that gets funny, I'm going to bust him up. If I have to break his neck, in my head I'm going to kill him. Then I'm going to justify myself, I'm a dirty cop, I'll fabricate, I'll get out of it, then they'll leave me alone."

Traumatized and culture shocked by his new and harsh reality, and forced to adapt to a gladiator environment of hardened criminals being ex-LAPD, Ruben was enrolled in a very deadly crash course for survival.

"I was aware of the street politics, because I was a gang cop, but I didn't know the fullness of the prison politics, how they had the structure, I was pretty ignorant of it."

"I'm from Mexico; me showing up to prison, I have to run Pices. If I'm a Southern California resident or gang member, I would run Sureno."

"When I first showed up to prison, the first two-three months, I was in the hole (solitary confinement). I was in the hole by myself in a single cell.

And the lieutenant didn't want to leave me in general population because of my background. But I told them I ain't got no worries, I ain't got no beef with anybody, I don't care, I don't want problems.

"I still had a lot of bad thoughts in my head, like I'm going to get even, all these guys betrayed me, told on me, I'm getting some bad thoughts in my head while I'm in the hole."

An Encounter with God, By an Ex-Hells Angel

"Then all of a sudden I get this ex-Hells Angel to become my cellmate. He's a Christian now. I start sharing things with him, and we are talking. I told him I was ready to go to hell. I never heard of Salvation, I never heard of the Gospel, nobody ever preached the Gospel to me. So I'm thinking, I already have done all this crazy stuff, there's no way to turn back, no way to change my ways, no way to get a second chance, no way to start over. In my head, I'm thinking, the only way to go is with a bang. So I'm thinking in my head, 'what's the point of being good, if there's no reward, there's nothing there for me?'

"He tells me that I can get out of hell, I don't have to go to hell, you can get a second chance, you can get your life right and you can get your Salvation. And he starts preaching the Gospel to me. And I'm grateful to God that he opened my heart up. Hearing that word of Hope, faith came into my heart.

"I listened because I wanted to know if it was real and true. I had never heard it and to me I was lost, so messed up, angry and bitter to the point where the only way out was to go out with a bang. In my mind, I'm thinking when I get out of this place, I'm going to walk out and get even and who cares if they take me out. I'm still going down anyways. I might as well take anyone I can with me. In my head, I was so messed up with PTSD, that I felt that was the way to go."

Prison Politics

"I had no clue what was up ahead, I thought everything is good, I'm saved, I'm right with God, next thing you know they take me out the hole and put me in general population. So now I'm open to the general population.

"I'm excited about God, I'm not thinking about nothing, I'm ready to go serve God in prison, no fear, nothing. I'm not even thinking about the politics. When I show up to the general population, I'm there, the first day is good, the second day I met two other Christians, we're reading the Bible together, we're sharing the Lord and I'm just thinking about Jesus and what He is doing.

Then all of a sudden, I get confronted by the Southerners (Surenos/Mexican Mafia), the shot callers. They tell me that I got to leave because I'm an ex cop. I'm like 'prove it.' I said, ' I'm not going nowhere.' Then all of a sudden the violent, angry mentality kicks in, I'm thinking 'these punks aren't going to tell me what to do' and I said. 'I'm not going nowhere man. I said, 'I'm not going to go by myself, we are all going to go together."

"Then I told them, ' I'm a Christian now, I'm trying to get my life right, I'm trying to change.' I said, 'I don't want no problems.'"

Ruben pauses and then tells me, "So then, I'm going to give God all the glory, because I believe this was all perfected by God, because when I'm there, the shot caller was from a neighborhood that I grew up around and his shot caller, his boss on the street, was my friend. I used to train him in boxing. So I tell him, 'hey, do me a favor. Call Chief, you know Chief?, he says, 'yeah that's my homeboy, I said, 'well call him up.' So when he calls him, I guess Chief cleaned me up and they left me alone. I was able to stay there two years in general population, preaching and learning and getting deep into the Word of God.

Redemption of a Rogue LAPD Cop

A young Ruben Palomares, right.

The youth center in East L.A. where Ruben trained.

Redemption of a Rogue LAPD Cop

Boxing Coach Al Spanky

Ruben worked as a tactics and self-defense trainer with Gene Lebell, left.

Ruben with fellow inmates.

Chapter 7

Spiritual Warfare

During those two years, Ruben is growing spiritually strong in the Lord and during this spiritual growth process, God is showing him the inner areas of his heart and soul that had been wounded by the various trauma throughout his turbulent and violent life. He begins to show Ruben through His Word that there is much inner spiritual healing to be done, because in those inner wounds of the soul, demons can hide-out and work their assignment and curses to manifest in an individual's life, even a Christian.

Ephesians 4:27 tell us, not to give place to the devil. Unresolved trauma can cause roots of bitterness, unforgiveness, pride, hatred, etc. During this time, there would be an incident after his Salvation which would startle him and bring him to the realization that there were still demons living within him, which were given legal housing, through him giving place to unresolved sin and trauma.

"And that's when the real deep spiritual warfare things start happening. One day, I'm still talking with my ex who has my daughters and I get into a big old argument with her on the phone and I want to cuss, I want to lash out, and I'm thinking, 'whoaaa, where did that come from?' I thought I was a Christian, I thought I was supposed to be all holy and good. I didn't know that stuff still happened. So I started talking to God about it. I said, 'Lord, I don't understand this. Why do I still have this anger in me, this rage inside me, which makes me want to hurt people still?

"In my mind I'm thinking once you've given your life to Christ, you read the Bible, everything's supposed to be good, you're good to go, you're changed, you're not going to do nothing crazy any more, you're going to be good. I wasn't aware of what was going to happen to me next. The spiritual warfare starts.

Attacked by Demons

The Bible clearly states in Ephesians Chapter 6, that we do not wrestle against flesh and blood, we wrestle against demonic stir. It's a structured spiritual army. It does exist, you might not see it physically, because they're going to keep themselves in the dark so you don't see them, so you don't prepare yourself and know how to go against them.

When you look around, and the evil, the violence that you see, all the stuff that's going on in this world, there's some demonic and spiritual influence behind it, on the good and the bad side. There's no equality when it comes to spiritual warfare. God is almighty, the enemy (satan) is way under His feet, but we as humans aren't aware of that, so we give into that stuff.

Ruben reflects back on his first paranormal demonic attack when he began reading a book titled, "Thou Shall Cast Out Demons," by Demon Deliverance Minister Derrick Prince.

"I read the whole book and in the back there is a long prayer. Praise God for that prayer, because when I'm sitting in my cell by myself, on a chair, I pray the whole prayer. It tells you how to renounce curses, how to break curses, how to get rid of the occult influence, and me going to that witch, I opened the door to a curse.

"When I prayed this prayer, I felt something evil and nasty come out of me. I felt something pull me and come out of me, and it freaked me out. I felt it come out of my whole body, from out of my chest like a pressure, it pulled away from me, really heavy. It was terrible, but it was awesome at the same time. But when it left, I felt this lightness, this weight came off of me, I was like whoaaaa. Praying in the name of Jesus, the authority comes from Jesus, the victory comes from Jesus."

Demonic Voices In My Head

In addition to the physical demonic attacks, Ruben was also having numerous voices manifest in his head. Ruben explains:

"Let's say when you're going through something difficult, during that time they'll amplify the thoughts and voices that are going to torment you. Let's say in my case, I started hearing a lot of rumors about my case, how much time they want to give me. I started getting more tormented by those voices.

"You're not going to get out," "You're going to get life," Ruben says the voices were telling him--"and I'm being freaked out."

"Sometimes I would say verses of the Bible and I would feel them getting mad. They would say, "Stop saying that." I would say, "I overcame by the blood of the lamb and the word of my testimony (Revelation 12:11), and I would say verses about the enemy's final judgement, the lake of fire, and they didn't like that, it would affect them bad. I could feel them stop bugging me.

The Bible is the Word of God, you might have psychologists and psychiatrists give you mental wisdom, but they haven't touched into the spiritual realm to understand that there is more behind the scenes.

Ruben's spiritual battle would intensify when he is transferred back to San Bernardino County to face more charges.

"In 2003, I get moved to the county jail into the hole in San Bernardino County, because now I have a second indictment, because all the co-defendants of mine open up the other stuff that I was doing, so now I got two indictments and I'm waiting to get sentenced on that one, and I'm in the hole (two years have passed). But I'm already thinking I'm squared away, I'm a solid Christian. But when I'm in the hole now, I start reading more books on deliverance and deep inner healing stuff.

"I start experiencing some heavy duty demonic manifestations. And I'm like 'What's going on, I thought they were gone.' I'm thinking the first prayer cleared me up and I was ready to go."

"There was a time when I was praying and I would start feeling them come over me again. I'm like what's going on around here? I can feel an evil weight over me. So then I start feeling some pricks in my side. Boom, boom, like somebody's poking my ribs and I'm laying in my bunk and somebody's suffocating me again. I start praying, "Get off of me in the name of Jesus,' 'Leave me alone in the name of Jesus.'" And they would leave and come back. But now I'm feeling a tormenting inside, it's like all hell broke loose inside me. I went through a process for maybe like two weeks, nonstop constant torment, beat down throughout the day. Throughout the night, it was hardcore, come and go, come and go."

Generational Curses

"When I started reading the Bible, I started questioning God about this. 'Lord why did these family members die so young, why such a tragic death?'"

"I had to go to a lot of funerals growing up, a lot of them were my uncles and cousins, young ones. One of my uncles was fixing his lowrider when I was about 7, 6 years old, and the jack broke and crushed his head, killed him. One of his other brothers about four to five years later shot himself in the heart, killed himself. His dad was waiting for the bus one day, and had like a seizure, fell out and hit his head on the sidewalk and went into a coma and then died."

"My family, we were raised Catholic, but we didn't read the Bible growing up. We just believed what they told us, we were into religion/cult stuff. My grandmother was raised Catholic, but she also went to witches. Someone had cursed her, so she would go to witches to get a cleaning, a limpia, and that alone would open up a curse in her life and a generational curse in the bloodline, by her own practices.

My grandmother and her husband practiced witchcraft too, and one of my aunts, so there was a curse in the family.

Demonic Attacks Increase

That generational curse, along with the curses Ruben was afflicted with along the journey of his own life, would manifest in Hollywood horror fashion in his cell at the San Bernardino County Jail.

"One day I'm laying on my bunk, I feel something choking me and smothering my face, I don't see nobody, nobody's physically there. It felt like a 50-pound pillow smothering my face and something was strangling my neck. I was not on dope, I didn't use drugs, I stopped smoking that weed years ago. I started telling them to stop in the name of Jesus, I started exercising the name of Jesus and it left.

Ruben said they would, leave and come back. These attacks would be ongoing, throughout the day and night. Ruben was frustrated and perplexed. He was a Born Again Christian. He would keep asking God, 'why is this still happening?' He didn't realize at the time, that this was all a part of God's divine plan for his life and ministry.

Chapter 8

On the Path to God's Inner Healing & Demon Deliverance

"I started taking this course, Transformation of the Inner Man by Elijah House. In this course, they have prayers and as I'm doing these prayers for deliverance, that's when things started getting released inside me. That's when I started feeling the strong demonic presence. I started freaking out so bad, because I couldn't stop it, no matter how many verses I quoted, I'm getting real frustrated, desperate. I'm like 'Lord please help me, I don't know what I'm going to do.' I really felt God saying, 'reach out and get in touch with the body of Christ.'"

Ruben noticed in the back of the book there was contact information for some deliverance ministries. After a long period of waiting patiently, which seemed like an eternity, Ruben recalls.

"Finally, some deliverance ministers show up there from Deep Healing Ministries. They have three or four prayers warriors in the parking lot while they're praying for me."

The Holy Spirit told them to come see me, they never went to a prison. They told me, 'We never been to any jails or prisons, but when I got your note, I really, clearly felt the Lord telling me to come see you, come pray for you, you're going through some demonic harassment' and I said, 'wooow, thank you Jesus.'

"The first session, we got into this conversation of what's going on, and they did this first prayer, and I really felt lighter, better, I felt good. So I'm thinking, thank God, I hope this is it.

They leave, I go back to the cell. I'm in a single cell, (five years in the hole at that time), around nothing but lifers, Eme (Mexican Mafia), Aryan Brothers. So, when I'm there, I start sensing it's still going on, but it's not as strong, but it's still going on, I'm thinking, 'What the heck? When's it going to stop?' I'm praying to God, 'Lord, why is this taking so long, why am I having to go through all this harassment?'"

How People Open Spiritual Doors for Demons

"I thought it was going to be over with, with these prayer sessions. Little did I know that because, due to so many of the doors I opened through my PTSD, shootings, through my abuse, my violence, my hatred, my unforgiveness and sexual immorality, there was layers and layers that the Lord had to peel and he wanted to do it one at a time, he wasn't going to do it all at one time."

Ruben explains how demons can legally gain authorization in the spirit realm to place curses on humanity:

"If I'm practicing sin and I'm violating God's laws, it's giving the enemy rights to basically harass me to mess with my life."

Ruben now explains how curses are broken, through the power of God's Word:

"You renounce it, you ask for forgiveness and you repent for it. You turn away from it. I'm going to stop going back to that practicing sin. Let's just say it was lust, being a fornicator, I'm going to have to ask for forgiveness for that, I'm going to renounce it, and I'm going to repent of it, I'm going to turn away from it, I'm going to stop going back to that practicing sin."

"Same thing if I'm using drugs, it's an addiction. It's a destructive thing that's going to hurt you, it's going to destroy your life and not let you fulfill God's purpose for your life."

"You cracked the door open somehow, it could've been through some childhood event, it could've been just to fit in, you start smoking weed and it starts going to deeper stuff."

Breaking the Chains through Forgiveness
"And when ye stand praying, forgive, if ye have ought against any: that your Father also which is in heaven may forgive you your trespasses." Mark 11:25

"You can forgive everyone that hurt you, even if they abused you, beat you, whatever the case may be, but if you haven't forgiven yourself, you're still going to bound up, you're going to give the enemy legal right to harass you and keep the strongholds inside you."

"He was working on me at the same time, what it was doing was building my relationship and my trust with God stronger. It was also allowing me to experience His presence and love more and allowing me to understand how important I was to Him."

"It also helped me to understand other people too. I was so judgmental before, I was such a self-righteous individual before. I hated everybody. All of a sudden I'm looking at people that at one time I wanted to beat up and shoot, I'm loving them, I'm seeing them different. God is working in me, I'm thinking, I can't believe I was this person, and if some issue would come up, I would say, 'Lord, why did I feel that way towards this person?'"

"The beautiful part of this was, the Lord was dealing with my rooted issues, the deep level healing, they (demons) were having to release legal rights. They were leaving, they were leaving just one at a time and it was awesome, I could feel the difference."

Prison Evangelist

God would commission Ruben to become a prison evangelist. Ruben was a type of modern day Saul of Tarsus. As told in the New Testament (Acts:9), Saul, a dedicated persecutor of Christians, a number one enemy of Christ, would be transformed by a supernatural appearance of Christ on the road to Damascus. He would become a Christian, however initially he was still feared and not trusted by many Christians, due to his notorious history.

This would somewhat parallel with Ruben's story, who was now on a mission from God to share the Gospel to convicted criminals and gang members, the very demographic he would unjustly persecute and place in prison. Saul who was renamed Paul by Jesus, would eventually gain the trust and respect of his new peers and become Christianity's most noted leader in spreading the Gospel of Jesus Christ throughout the nations.

Ruben was now by the grace and mercy of God doing likewise, however within the prison setting.

"I've experienced supernatural miracles, I experienced supernatural deliverances. We are in prison and me and some other brothers pray for somebody and the Lord heals them of a cancer. The Holy Spirit starts using us to pray in tongues, and supernaturally we feel the power of God come upon us. You cannot confuse God's presence, it's so powerful, so peaceful, it just overwhelms you. It's like the best high in the world. It's the best experience you can ever have, to be in His presence and when He's there and when you're praying in tongues to Holy Spirit, it just comes upon you, sometimes it just breaks you down, you just start tearing up. It's a supernatural event and you know you're not alone; you know God is there for you, you know He's real, and you know He really loves you."

God was utilizing Ruben as a traveling evangelist in the prison system, ministering deliverance and inner healing in prison, setting the captives free. In his 16 years in prison, he was able to do prison ministry in California, Texas and Arizona.

"In prison, there are so many hurt and wounded people there, I started asking God to use me, 'I'm here Lord, use me.' I was around lifers too, in the hole, and I would preach to them and pray healing and deliverance over them."

"I'm in a new prison in Fort Worth Texas. When I show up, there are 1,900 people there in that prison. There's a lot of different politics-- prison politics, gang politics. When I show up, I go to the Mexican shot callers and I tell them who I am, my name and what I'm there for. Right away when you go to prison, the races are going to hit you up. They think I'm white, so the white boys are going to hit me up. They're going to ask me where I'm from, who I'm running with and right away I say, 'I'm a Christian, I run with the Lord and I'm also Mexican.'

So I go to the Mexican shot callers and I tell them 'Look, I'm a Christian, but I am Mexican, I don't run the politics stuff, but I do serve the Lord and I am in prison for this reason. I tell them why I am in prison.

"Because I believe this. I say, 'Look Lord, If I'm going to represent you in here, I'm in here, this is where I do my time, where I program the way you want me to do. I can't be doing it hiding and acting like nothing happened, I messed up and I'm going to serve you in here. But if I go in there and start pretending that I'm in here for tax evasion and they find out, they are going to say that I'm a coward.'

"Well I figure it like this, the worse they can do to me, they can try to jump me or beat me up or send me to the hole, I say I ain't worried about it, I'm a fast runner," Ruben says with a smile.

"I'm not trying to fight no more Lord, I'm tired of fighting. The Bible says in Proverbs 16:7, 'When a man's ways please the Lord, even his enemies are at peace with him." And I believe Him for that, because it's true. Every yard I went to, the Surenos are the gang members that would probably hate me the most, because I was a gang cop from Southern California, and the gang unit. I dealt with the 18th Streeters, the M.S., the biggest gangs out there, but the Lord would give me favor with them, I even played softball with them."

When Ruben would meet a new group of inmates, in a new yard or institution, he said he would tell them,

'I'm not here to fight, I'm not here to gang bang, I'm here to bring Christ to you guys, I just want to do my time' and they just left him alone.

"Of course you're going to have guys behind your back hating on you, talking crazy. I told the Lord, 'Look, you deal with those guys.'"

"If I started feeling some ill feelings towards somebody, because I heard them talking behind my back, the enemy (satan) would want me to smack that guy, I would say, "Lord, I forgive that guy, and help me not hate him, help me not hold anything against him. This guy, he doesn't know any better, and I would just move on and be about my business."

"So I worked for the chaplain there and he started bringing me some of the guys who had PTSD. He brought a former police officer, ;lieutenants, military, he brought me child molesters, gang members, people that really wanted to change and get help. He would bring them to me and I would say, 'Lord, you brought them to me Lord, I'm not going to deny nobody, I'm going to see them the way you want me to see them, I'm here for them."

"And they respected me, and why? Because they knew the Lord was working through me."

Ruben talks about his initial resistance to minister to child molesters:
"The enemy tried to distract me and say, 'I hate those dudes,' but I said 'Lord, I'm suppose to love everybody, I love everybody and forgive me if I have any thoughts that don't come from you. Put those people in my path so I can pray for them. If you heal them and you deliver them Lord, they're going to be able to minister to other people with their situation.'"

"I have delivered guys that were under a curse, they were from the cartel, they got cursed by a girlfriend and I've seen them get delivered. I've seen the demons manifest inside them and they didn't believe in that stuff either."

I asked Ruben how they would manifest.
"They start having like seizures, contorting, the body's moving. You know it's nothing normal, it's supernatural and it's not good, and the person's freaking out, doing some weird moves in his body, from that his eyes roll back, you see all kinds of stuff.

When you pray in the name of Jesus, the person you're renouncing the curses on, you see their body go limp and drop. He's telling you, 'well I've never believed in this stuff, I'm delivered, I feel it.' That person was a cartel killer, crazy dude and now he's got the Bible under his armpit and won't let it go, because he knows there's two forces at war, but he knows the powerful force is Jesus. That curse is gone, they can't go against Him (Jesus). The only way they hurt the Lord is to hurt humans, because they can't hurt Him."

I asked Ruben if he'd discipled anyone who is now discipling others.

"Right now as a matter of fact, one of my Christian brothers in there who got 14 years was the former lieutenant. for the SWAT Team in San Francisco, who was an atheist. He's actually doing Bible studies out there now. The Lord is using him to do deliverance and deep level healing. So the Lord used me to equip him. He's got a Theology Master's now and he was atheist before. He was going to kill himself before, he was suicidal.

"The chaplain brought him to me, he says, 'hey I want you to talk to this guy, he's been going to the psychologist for two years, nightmares, flashbacks, PTSD.'

I asked Ruben what turned him around.

"The Holy Spirit," he answered.

"We had three sessions and each session the Lord would move and cause results. The Lord would move and heal him. And this person is doing great. He's doing Bible studies, they moved him to another prison in Lompoc. His wife wrote and said that he's actually doing Bible studies now, the chaplain approved the classes on the topic of deliverance and inner healing.

Why is Deliverance and Inner Healing So Vital?

"And these signs shall follow them that believe; In my name shall they cast out devils; they shall speak with new tongues;" Mark 16:17

"It's the children's bread" (Matthew 15:26). "The Lord that created us, knows what's wrong with each of us. "If you don't get that deliverance, You're going to be harassed, tormented, you're going to be stuck, you're not going to able to get through the rut. You need deliverance, you really need it."

God's Divine Grace, Mercy & Forgiveness For All of Us

Ruben explains God's divine forgiveness once an individual receives His son Jesus Christ as their Lord and Savior (John 3:16, Romans 10:9):

"Your record (sin) is under the blood. You're clean, you're forgiven, you're redeemed. Your spirit is new, your spirit is one with Christ now, you're one with the Holy Spirit, but what you don't know is that your soul and your fleshly mind still has attachments, harassments, open doors. The Bible says, 'the Word of God has to renew your mind and also transform you (Romans 12:2) and at the same time you need the deliverance, because that's where the enemy could be attached to you.

The Bible says in your anger, do not sin, don't give room to the devil, the enemy (Ephesians 4:26-27). But if you have been a prideful, angry individual and you opened doors to the enemy and you come to Christ, you don't know that behind the scene those spirits are right there harassing you. You can be a loving Christian, but that anger can control you, and you don't know, that that's a demonic force right there."

Chapter 9

Ruben's Mission Now as a Free Man

"I see the Lord opening up doors for me to go back and preach to police officers, because they need the Lord. If you have good leaders, they will help the communities heal and then people will respect them. People will see Christ in these leaders and they will respect the police officers. But also reach out to the gang members, to our communities out there, and do a outreach program to help people and educate people and share the Lord."

Ruben's Words of Advice

"My advice would be, don't lose your hope, don't get discouraged, the Bible is true, the Bible does talk about the enemy (satan), it is real, there is answers, solutions, you have to seek the Body of Christ, there's a lot of members in the body of Christ that are equipped and blessed by God that care about you, that love you, and want to help you, but don't be afraid, don't think you're the only one going through it, you're not alone.

There are so many members that have been through it, been there, done that and can help you. Don't think you're the only one, don't think you're alone, don't think God doesn't love you, don't think God's not there for you. The enemy wants you to believe that lie. There's so many people there to help you, you got to reach out. Don't lose hope."

Basic Prayer of Salvation & Deliverance

For God so loved the world, that he gave his only begotten Son, that whosoever believeth in him should not perish, but have everlasting life.
John 3:16

God is a loving and forgiving God who delights in His creation. In his word He says, "For I know the thoughts that I think toward you, saith the Lord, thoughts of peace, and not of evil, to give you an expected end."
Jeremiah 29:11

Now think of the goodness of Yeshua... and repeat this prayer out loud...

Father, I decree your son Yeshua Hamashia as Lord and Savior over every area of my life. I believe Father, that your son Yeshua Hamashia was placed on the cross for my sins and the world's sins, and that He was buried and raised by You on the Third Day. I repent for all my sins (name them) and for my ancestors' sins on my mother and father's side, known and unknown. I ask your forgiveness for all my sins and I forgive all those who have offended me and sinned against me. I forgive myself.

Redemption of a Rogue LAPD Cop

I renounce all demonic activity that I have participated in my past and my present, I renounce, reject and repent this day for all:

- Witchcraft, Sorcery, Black Magic, White Magic, and Divination

- Pharmakia (Witchcraft through Drugs)

- Horoscope, new age, yoga, psychic readings, etc.

- Tarot cards and palm readings, and all cultic practices which pay homage to pagan eastern religions.

- Ouija Boards

- Worldly music and entertainment which pays respect and glamorizes evil lifestyles.

- Prayers to false gods and spirit guides.

- Membership in secret societies, Greek letter organizations, Freemasons, etc.. all organizations that give honor to false gods.

- Gang ties (name your gang)

- Soul ties-current and past, and all demonic unions created through fornication and occult sex magic and perversions.

- I renounce all demonic covenants, soul ties and portals to the soul, created through drugs, alcohol, strange tattooing and strange piercings.

By the power of the blood of Yeshua, I break off every curse, hex, spell, soul tie, curse words people have spoken, generational curses of disease, sickness, premature death, depression, addictions, mental illness, anger, murder, divorce, gangs, violence, poverty, sexual perversion, witchcraft, abuse, abandonment, idolatry, jealousy, unforgiveness, pride, social life problems, _____,_____ in every area of my life. I call now the fire of the Holy Spirit (Hebrews 10:29) to burn and torment every demonic spirit hiding within my conscious and subconscious mind, emotions, body, tattoos, symbols, home, etc.. I command the Holy Ghost fire in Yeshua's name to burn them out of their hiding places now!!!

Angels of the Lord bind the demonic king and queen ruling over any area of my life and put a fiery chain around the neck of the head demon or principality who received the assignment from satan to afflict, torment, oppress, and possess me, and a chain of fire around every evil spirit under the authority of the principality.

Break their demonic crowns off their heads, along with all their jewelry, amulets, and any devices and weapons they came with on their assignment.

I command these spirits to pack their belongings right now and prepare to leave my body and soul. My soul, being, my emotions, will, and conscious and subconscious mind. Leave my home and family in Yeshua Hamashia's name... Now!!!. I say out in the name of Yeshua!!!

Angel of the Lord, drag these spirits and every spirit under their authority into the outer darkness into the Abyss. Evil spirits, I command you never to return again.Yeshua, I ask you now to close every portal of my soul, that has been open to the demonic world through the sorcery I've done through drugs, alcohol, sexual promiscuity, worship of demons and false gods, generational curses, occult magic, gangs, pagan secret societies, witchcraft, etc., and the spirits which have haunted my mind with tormenting thoughts, voices, hallucinations, nightmares, demonic paranormal experiences, sickness
and disease, etc..

I thank you for the blood of your son Yeshua, I decree right now that it protects and covers me from the enemy. I thank you Yeshua for the stripes that you allowed to be torn violently in your back, for Your
Word states in 1 Peter 2:24, "By His stripes we are healed." So I decree that by Yeshua's stripes, I'm healed, from the top of my head to the soles of my feet.

Father, Your Word says in Romans 10:13, "Whosoever that call on the name of the Lord, shall be Saved." and John 8:36 states, "Who the Son has set free, is free indeed." So I call on you, Yeshua Hamashia as my Lord and Savior, and I decree by Your Word that I'm set free indeed!!!

Father, I ask that you fill me now with your Holy Spirit. Acts 1:8 states that I will receive power when I receive the Holy Spirit and that He will lead me into all Truth according to John 16:3. I receive this Holy impartation by faith and the gifts that accompanies it, such as the gift of speaking in new tongues, among others which is referenced in scripture according to 1 Corinthians Chapter 12.

Redemption of a Rogue LAPD Cop

Lord, I ask you to give me the discernment of every skill-set, talent and spiritual gifts you have placed within me, so I can utilize them to win souls and bring you glory. I decree by faith that your Holy Spirit is leading me now towards Your perfect will, plan and purpose for my divine destiny in Christ's Kingdom.

I decree that I have the mind of Christ according to 1 Corinthians 2:16 and the divine armor of God according to Ephesians 6, which is the helmet of salvation, breastplate of righteousness, belt of truth, sword of the spirit (which is the Word of God), and that my feet are prepared with the Gospel of Christ. I decree that I and my family are blessed in Yeshua Hamashia's name.

So be it!!!!

Praise God!!!

*Please share your testimonies
with us @ ThugExposed.org,
by mailing them to:*

*ThugExposed.Org
1026 Florin Road #171
Sacramento, CA 95831*

or email me @ rayfordjohnson@me.com.

Made in the USA
Coppell, TX
28 February 2026

72620672R00042